How to MAKE MONEY in any economy;

The Secret to taking advantage of Population Numbers with practical examples.

By

IFEANYI UBAH

My most Profound gratitude goes to

Jesus Christ; My King and God

I dedicate this book

To

My family.

My friends.

Everyone willing to make MONEY in any economy.

This book is a collection of my observations, researches and perceptions on wealth creation as well as lessons learnt on my journey to RICHES.

This book was also borne out of my sheer determination to eliminate the poverty of the mind; the dragon-headed monster that has inhibited your ability to create and distribute wealth and to prove to you that you really have no permanent obstacle in the journey to MAKING CASH.

This Book is divided into;

1. Introduction.

1

Introduction

- Everything is in the numbers. Everything can be measured in the numbers -

The great Pythagoras is the initiator of this thought that still holds true today. Some might argue that so many things are uncountable, which is quite obvious but one thing is clear; they can still be measured in the numbers. For example: *"the one thousand, seven hundred Waterfalls of Canada"*. My point here is this: whether countable or uncountable, everything is and can be measured in the numbers which is an important factor in understanding the playgrounds navigated by true wealth.

Population is simply the number of something in a particular place. It is very safe to say that Human population is the number of humans in a particular place. Population is wealth if optimized. Population is of enormous value. Population number can be the catalyst for rapid cash-in-flow. Democracy also rightly aligns with the more populated as it tells us that *"majority carries the vote"*.

In recent times, especially with the launch of the social media, your population following (followers) can catapult you to a near-stress less financial freedom in comparison to previous ages. Remember this: population is Money, Population is overwhelmingly valuable, Population is the new gold, Population is audience, Population is hungry and you *gotta* feed it to stay or remain on top.

Anybody adept at converting any given population number to money, will have a very sustainable cash-in-flow system as long as he continues to not only quench their hunger flames but strives to satiate them. The game of football is one underrated case-study of how population numbers can pleasantly embarrass you with stupendous wealth. A lot of youngsters are seriously cashing out.

Everyone wants to make money and it is usually the desire that drives people onto personal finance. On a daily, I hear statements like *"money no dey, wetin man go do, economy too hard, everywhere dey tight now, e get as things be......"* These comments most times reflect the hopeless state of people who expect to be living in financial bliss but unfortunately, are not anywhere near that realm.

However, this is not to say you cannot make money in any economy. You can in fact make money at the 'expense' of the population. I mean you can cash out big time with the population as your primary conduit.

The Major principle I try to emphasize in all of the chapters is the visible success enjoyed by the 'Otherish' Givers. According to Adam Grant, Author of Give and Take, *"there are three kinds of people in the World; The Givers, Takers and Matchers"*. He further classified givers into 'selfless' Givers and 'Otherish' Givers. Of the two, Otherish givers are more successful and stay at the top of the ladder.

Selfless givers, as you may presume, are the ones who drop everything they are engaged with to help people all the time, which means they tend to fall behind on their own work. They constantly do things to their own detriments and therefore end up at the bottom of the success ladder; though they're still much happier people than the takers.

On the other side, Otherish givers are smart and strategic about their giving. While they're just as much givers as their counterparts; the selfless givers, they've learned to successfully cruise a world where matchers and takers reside, so others don't take undue advantage of them.

Giving well is about keeping an eye on interests

Source: *conversationagent.com*

In every Clime, there is a rich combo of takers and matchers. Givers on the other hand are always a tiny portion of the population anywhere in the World. The major difference between them all is seen in their varying abilities to channel attention and energy on making a difference in the lives of people.

Sadly, people cannot MAKE CASH when they ignore the opportunities to be givers and distributors of value. Takers can never ever rise above givers as long as the socio-economic ladder is concerned. Find something to give or distribute to a large segment of the population and wait for the cash to flow in.

The financial destiny of any Country or Continent hovers around the exceptional ability of its people to create, sell, give, refine and distribute value. Africa distributes value but Africa has largely been on the receiving end.

Givers, especially 'Otherish' givers are actively engaged in this process. Hence, their tall standing among the pack cannot be disputed. They exhibit classic mastery in the creation and the distribution of value. The core of their actions is in their capability to distribute or redistribute payable value to a greater chunk of the population.

-Value distributed is directly proportional to cash inflow-

-Sometimes, the value created can be indirectly proportional to cash inflow based on the factor of scale and expansion-

I cannot categorically say that I am an authority in Wealth Creation but one thing I know for sure is that making cash in any economy cannot be attained if you don't understand the dynamics that attract them. I will show you how to on this remarkable journey.

Kindly bear in mind that this whole book is based on the concept of the 'Otherish' Giver.

2

Tolaram's Model

One of the most inspiring business stories about leveraging population numbers in Making Cash is the model being operated by the Tolaram Group.

History and Origin

Tolaram Group is a Singapore based conglomerate with a major presence in West Africa. They journeyed into Nigeria in 1976, and never looked back.

They debuted in Nigeria as a trading company but quickly expanded into manufacturing and marketing of textiles, industrial goods and electronics, before moving on to concentrate on consumer goods. Their success story in Fast Moving Consumer Goods (FMCG) began in 1988 when they first introduced instant noodles to the Nigerian taste bud. Noodles were an unfamiliar product in the country as at the time but that proved to be a competitive advantage due to their deep understanding of local consumer taste preferences.

Kindly note that they launched an entirely new product into the market when they understood the choices of the local consumer; the choice on the kind of items with values to be purchased and the choice on the price of the item. It is therefore right to deduce that;

Understanding of customers' preferences informed the launch of the instant noodles into the Nigerian market.

Over time, the business flourished and from serving the market through imports, three noodle manufacturing facilities were set up, giving them a strong footing to remain as market leaders. They had understood the psychology of consumers and their overall preferences relative to products marketed to them; they had tested the waters; it was time to sail to the dockyard for a sustainable business setting had been discovered.

You can only make cash when you know your customer. You can make multiple streams of cash when you create and distribute value to a large chunk of the population. This is the Otherish giving method.

In his article titled, *how one Company defied the odds and is growing almost $1 Billion in revenue in Nigeria* posted on the medium platform and the She Leads Africa's blog, Efosa Ojoma, co-author of the prosperity paradox talked about Tolaram's entry into Nigeria's business scene in spite of the prevalent anti-business realities. "Nigeria was not a choice investment destination when the Company kicked off operations in 1988; Life expectancy for Nigeria's 91million people = 46 years; gross domestic product

(GDP) was about $23 billion; GDP per capital was about $253; 78% of the population lived on less than $2 per day; about 37% of people had access to sanitation while roughly 58% had access to improved water source; Nigeria had experienced six coups in its short 28 years of existence as a republic; political instability ". These were very conspicuous red flags that would have convinced even the bravest of hearts that Nigeria, as at the time, seemed to be a 'Bermuda triangle' for any business investment.

Business Model

He went further to say that Executives at the Tolaram Group paid little or no attention to the statistics above. In fact, they started importing instant noodles into Nigeria in 1988. They came with a mission to target non-consumption. The Company's vision was to bring affordability and quality to the low socio-economic segments in the Country. They sold their products for as little as 10 cents as at the time.

Essentially, the business model of the Tolaram's Group borders on **Acceptability, Affordability** and **Accessibility**.

Please, do not get this wrong, lots of businesses in Africa or anywhere in the world can primarily function to address the needs of the class high up the socio-economic ladder. Yet, to leverage on the mass population as a conduit for making cash, you must be willing to sell a product or service that can be easily purchased (affordability) with disposable income; that has the necessary channels of distribution of the product to the eventual consumers (accessibility); that satisfies a desire or need (acceptability).

In her Medium article titled, *the mystery of market size in Nigeria*, Dr. Ola Brown, founder of the Nigerian flying doctors, wrote on the 6 things to think about when innovating for scale in the Nigerian Market. Two of the 6 points that align with this book's context are:

1. Understand the size of the Market that you are targeting, their needs and most importantly their capacity to pay.
2. Stop innovating for your friends and start innovating for your gateman; most Nigerians are poor, very poor. Find the price point that they can afford.

In other words, as a business owner or an aspiring one, whenever you decide to set up or expand your business to reach a wider customer base, you need to have a very deep understanding of your target market, their needs and their willingness to pay for your products and services.

William Ukpe, @William_Ukpein's tweet on the 20th of August gave credence to the need for business people to offer an ingenious value that can make their target market part ways with money.

He said, "Anyone that tells you Entrepreneurship can save Nigeria is lying to you. You cannot Entrepreneur your way to prosperity if the business environment is 'shit'.

Secondly, when only 8% of your population is considered middle Class, starting a business is an extreme sport. To make matters worse, in the 8% that falls under the middle class, they spend 60% of their income on food. Meaning your target market has 'shit' to do with money.

@asemota has war stories of how coca cola learnt this the hard way when Nigerians started buying phone credit. Nigerians don't earn much, and Nigerians will prioritize their most important needs before your business.

Entrepreneurship can only come into play when the government has brought in inclusive economic reforms to bring in investments and decentralize control. Obasanjo's telecoms reforms have made more millionaires than 40 years of NITEL.

In 2018, Nigeria lost 43% of foreign direct investments (FDI). If investments are not coming, Nigerians will get poorer, and when people are poorer, they don't have disposable income to patronize your business. Already with the inevitable Naira devaluation coming soon, a lot more Nigerians are going to fall away from the middle class. Meaning more competition for entrepreneurs, meaning more failures, more stories that touch.

Sadly, our Igbo brothers know this; If you know the money the Emekas and the Nnamdis are making doing spare parts business from Angola to Mozambique, you will weep for the Nigerian market. When the businesses leave, it is a terrible sign, Igbo men are leaving......"

In summary, create a product or service that people will be willing to prioritize and pay for. The Tolaram's model represents businesses all over the world launching an unfamiliar product in uncertain realities. The homework of knowing your customer is the most essential to having a competitive advantage. Know your customer. Be an Otherish Giver; find high benefits for others, but at a lower cost to yourself.

3

Dangote's Model

The day I saw Dangote's truck in faraway India, it dawned on me that he had reached 'the ends of the World'. I looked on in utmost disbelief till the heavy-road vehicle sped off. Dangote has carved a niche for himself amongst the most profitable and enviable brands in Africa having broken continental and intercontinental barriers although the Republic of Benin has denied him entrance into their territory. They prefer to patronize China.

The Dangote brand is another success story of how to make cash leveraging on population numbers. According to world bank's 2017 report, Nigeria has a population of 190.9 million people and estimated to be 402 million people by 2050 according to the US census bureau.

History and Origin

Aliko Dangote was born on the 10th of April,1957. He is a Nigerian dollar billionaire and owner of the Dangote group; a multinational conglomerate with interests in commodities. As of January 2015, he had an estimated net worth of $18.6 billion making him the richest man in Africa and the 67th richest man in the world according to Forbes.

The Dangote group whose core business focus is to provide local value added products and services that meet the basic needs of the African population has grown by leaps and bounds and has presence in 18 African countries. The group which has a market capitalization of over $24 bn as at December, 2013 has four of its 13 subsidiaries listed on the Nigerian stock exchange. One of its subsidiaries; Dangote cement plc is the biggest listed company in West Africa and the first Nigerian company to join the Forbes global 2000 companies. The group started as a trading company before it branched off into the manufacturing of commodities; a feat which in my opinion gave him a competitive advantage.

Dangote's quick business growth from 1977 teaches us that there is something tangible to learn from him; a native business man with tentacles spread around Africa. As an apprentice under his uncle, who was also into commodity trading, he learnt the strings of business; if you must excel in business, you must be able to understand local needs as well as the purchasing power of consumers on a unit scale, that is, how much will a particular consumer be willing to part with in order to purchase your value offerings. I think that the concept of understanding the customer or consumer is an over-flogged issue.

His first foray was into Commodity trading from where he rose to manufacturing. The next challenge to overcome was to set up solid distribution channels to reach the customers; one of the most important assets in the group's value chain. Bear in mind that infrastructure development is too poor in Nigeria. Road freight and Logistics are nightmares. Dangote got trucks for goods transport.

This model informs us that Africa is full of opportunities that could yield ground breaking dividends if harnessed properly. Any pragmatic approach embarked on to understand the various strata of opportunities in Africa would be mind shattering. From food processing, manufacturing, media, steel, construction, telecoms, sports, agribusiness, banking, industry, power production, mineral and crude refining, tourism and even entertainment, Africa has enough material ingredients to create and distribute enduring wealth. Majority of the business interests of the richest people on the African Continent testifies to this. Interestingly too, tech is beginning to build solid business structures that has attracted several foreign direct and indirect investments into Africa. Technological companies are leveraging mobile internet penetration on the Continent to serve as many people as possible. Technology, as we know it, shatters boundaries.

Dangote Group's subsidiaries.

According to Dangote's website; "Dangote Group is one of Nigeria's most diversified business conglomerates with a hard – earned reputation for excellent business practices and products' quality with its operational headquarters in the bustling metropolis of Lagos, Nigeria in West Africa.

The Group's activities encompass:

- **Cement** – Manufacturing & Distribution
- **Sugar** – Manufacturing / Refining & Distribution
- **Flour & Semolina** – Milling & Distribution
- **Pasta** – Manufacturing & Distribution
- **Salt** – Refining & Distribution
- **Food Seasoning** – Production & Distribution of stock seasoning cubes
- **Vegetable Oil** – Refining & Distribution
- **Tomato Paste** – Manufacturing & Distribution
- **Crude Oil Refinery** – Refining & Distribution
- **Petrochemicals** – Refining & Distribution
- **Fertilizer** – Manufacturing & Distribution
- **Packaging Materials** – Manufacturing & Distribution
- **Logistics** – Port Management & Haulage"

Strategy

With a closer look at the Group's business activities or interests, you would observe that the most of them are within the most basic necessity of man; Food.
Man needs to survive irrespective of his socio-economic class as the struggle for survival is real. The

engines of our bodies are powered by food. Dangote's interests in Sugar, flour, semolina, pasta, salt, food seasoning, tomato paste and fertilizers answers to the growing demand for food.

As long as his customers continue to exist, the Dangote's brand will continue to tremendously survive. I could say this because I consider his competitors negligible for now. They could up their game in order to thrive and possess some portions of the market share in the nearest future. In the meantime, Dangote's triumph continues.

For you to make money by leveraging on population numbers, you have to stop asking, "how can I help myself?"
The better question to consider asking yourself or thinking about is, "how can I help people and help myself?" or "in what ways can I create and distribute value to people?" That is the mindset of the Otherish giver.
Money will flow in subsequently but be ready to amass as much as possible when it does. The more sustainable your solution to a problem is, the more wide-reaching and acceptable it can get.

Another angle to looking at the Dangote's model is in thinking about basic products or services whose needs are recurring and in high demand. What this literally means is, deal in products or services that people keep on looking for to purchase or consume;

Products and services people will most likely purchase first prior to considering any other item on their scale of necessities; Products or services that people place a premium on as necessary to their existence amass the attention of consumers.

Fast moving consumer goods (FMCG) like milk, meat, eggs, pasta, bakery, cereals, beverages, seafood, fruits, personal hygiene and cosmetics, medications, household appliances, mobile devices, computer, building materials, computer accessories, mobile data, mobile airtime and some kids' products are typical examples of products that sell every day. They are non-seasonal.

In his interview with Mo Ibrahim; Sudanese-British billionaire business man during the 2019 Ibrahim governance weekend, Dangote's advice to youths that are interested in making fast money was for them to venture into Agriculture. According to him, the market is and will always be there. Food and cash crops cultivation rewards handsomely and can be the life-wire of any economy by reason of the fact that the population of any nation depends on it. His $2 billion rice factory project would provide 150,000 direct jobs excluding indirect jobs which will be more impactful than the $12 billion oil refinery project.

Interestingly we have online platforms like farm crowdy, Thrive Agric, Farm Kart, Pork Money, E-farms which are all doing a great job democratizing food and animal production.

A South African entrepreneur asked Dangote at the same event the sectors he would advise people to get into if they were to start a business, he replied, Agriculture and ICT.

In an article on the good key words platform, "there are 5 types of products that people will always want to buy". Products were classified into;

1. Products that make or save money.
2. Products that help people learn.
3. Products that entertain.
4. Products that make life healthy and comfortable.
5. Products that saves time and effort.

Business operations around these products' classifications can help anyone make money by leveraging on population numbers. So, if you are thinking of creating massive value as a means to making money, you now have them on your fingertips. You can also take advantage of the growing penetration of the internet to reach massive population numbers. Money will be made. This is how the Otherish givers reason.

Nigeria is the best kept secret according to Dangote. In spite of the fact that he proceeded from a wealthy background, resting on his oars was never an option. He said that he never took a single vacation in his first 20 years of running the group; a lesson to budding entrepreneurs and business people that delaying gratification most times is necessary for deep-reaching business growth. He saw the immense opportunity to serve a large chunk of the population and immediately seized it. He secured a loan from his uncle. Business was so good that he repaid the loan in 3 months.

Times have changed. Today, a lot of financial service companies, micro-finance banks and peer to peer lending platforms have sprung up to support 'viable' business ventures. My point is, if you do not have a wealthy relative like Dangote had, you can leverage on the availability of these money lending institutions to kick start your business. Your business plans, future projections and revenue models should be ready when applying for funds. Angel investors; high net worth individuals are easily accessible via the internet and social media platforms, Venture Capital (VC) funds are becoming popular in recent times as well. Aside the afore mentioned ways to secure funding for your business, an aspiring business person can have joint venture arrangement to set up business operations.

For example, Mr A provides funds for the business while Mr B provides the expertise (tailoring skill) to run the business. At the end of the day, each party is settled based on prior documented agreements.

Documentation of agreements is necessary in every joint venture to protect each party's interests in case of litigations. Human beings can become unexpectedly volatile in issues relating to money, hence it is strongly advised that you do not undertake any joint venture without agreements and specifications of the terms, conditions, stakes, profit allocation and expected contributions from all parties. These are the basics.

Alhaji Aliko Dangote understands the Market, so should you.

In her Medium article titled, *the mystery of market size in Nigeria*, Dr. Ola Brown, founder of the Nigerian flying doctors rightly states that "the biggest Company on the Nigerian Stock exchange sells salt, sugar, pasta and cement. Within the next two years, he will be launching a Petrol Company. Not artificially intelligent petrol, not 3-d printed petrol. The ordinary type that J.D Rockefeller was selling 100 years ago. There seems to be a marked difference between market needs and what people are willing to pay for. Alhaji understands the market and therefore continues to win".

Dangote's crude oil refinery and petrochemical plant has graced the headlines of several global media outlets, not only because of its massive size, but also because the project is one that would transform Nigeria from a petroleum product import country to an exporter of same overnight. Self-sufficiency in petrol production would be attained. You can imagine the forex this laudable projects would channel into Nigeria.

When you get big in business, decide to grow bigger. This is one great lesson Dangote's strategic business decisions teaches us.

Millennial's Model

"From Baby Boomers and those that grew up at a time of dramatic social change, to Generation X and those that saw the dawn of the age of technology and then to the Millennials who were born into the age of information. A generation that has been described as lazy, narcissistic, entitled and unable to stay in one job, have also been described as the most purpose driven and potentially the most entrepreneurial of all previous generations" – Jordan Daykin.

This generation has been generally influenced by an increase and spread of communications, media, science and technologies. Never has a generation been so aware of their unlimited options, thanks to the internet. "Over half of millennials around the World would rather make $30,000 a year at a job they love and are enthused about than $100,000 a year at one they don't", according to Millennial Career, lifestyle and travel blogger, Hannah Becker.

With a multitude of possibilities at their finger-tips, digitally savvy millennials are using social media and the internet to build strong communities and a following of customers; population numbers.

According to Inc.com, the top 20 most influential millennial entrepreneurs all created an internet-based service. The future is still the internet. Long gone are the days of businesses solely focusing on revenues, financial rewards and profits, as 87 percent of millennials believe that the success of a business should be measured on its impact on the world. It is about 'balance', finding a gap in the market that is also fulfilling to the individual on a personal level. Mark Zuckerberg had claimed that Facebook was created to accomplish a social mission "To make the world more open and connected". Ben Silbermann believes that Pinterest will connect you with the most important things in your life.

Most millennials believe that making an impact in the world is much more important than any financial reward. There is hardly any millennial I see today who isn't bubbling with one entrepreneurial idea or the other. They are beginning to divert from the long standing status-quo of business people trying to make a whole lot of money eventhough their actions can alter or hurt eco-systems. Millennials are aggressively forming strong coalitions with other millennials to create a World that they have always dreamt of seeing. The older folks believe that millennials are deviating from the 'norm'. The norm is to get a job, work your way through the corporate ladder as the years go by eventhough job security may not be guaranteed. That's the 9-5 work routine. Right

By: Rieva Lesonsky in the article, *Millennials are rewriting the rules of work and entrepreneurship.*

before their very eyes, millennial entrepreneurs are rocking the world; demanding changes by their collective strengths and actions. Remote working, freelancing, flexible work times, co-working spaces and peer to peer funding have become terminologies associated with millennials today. There are some entrepreneurs that have captivated my attention in recent times. I giggle with joy when I come across them on the media or otherwise. I am fascinated about their abilities to bring ideas to life, execute and scale them until they become sustainable businesses whilst positively impacting the World and affecting many many people.

1. **Iyinoluwa Aboyeji:**

Source: *financialtechnologyafrica.com*

He is the co-founder of Andela, Flutterwave and the just recently launched, FutureAfrica. Since the launch of Andela, E, as he is known on twitter has been on the news creating sustainable companies that have massive reach; solving problems by leveraging on technology and making many investors wealthy. He is my millennial poster boy of Otherish givers. Flutterwave is an online payment technology solution.

Future Africa is a community in conversation for a better Africa.

Andela is a company that identifies and develops Software Developers and Engineers. It is a company that is actively involved in capacity building. Not frivolous capacity building that yields nothingness, as most political leaders are wont to doing from time immemorial. I refer to capacity building that equips people to overcome tech challenges, in this case.

The surest route to self-sufficiency of any continent is in its ability to build the capacity of its people. E is solving man-made problems that have plagued the African Continent as long as we can remember. Illiteracy, unemployment, poor educational facilities and infrastructure have been the most ravaging behemoths of struggling youths in Africa. By the collective determination of his team, they are being tackled aggressively.

" Andela is an African company that identifies and nurtures software developers. The company launched operations in Nigeria in May 2014, to help global companies overcome the severe shortage of skilled software developers and has offices in Nigeria, Kenya,

Rwanda, Uganda and the United States" - Wikipedia

"Andela is a four-year technical leadership program focused on unlocking the full potential of Africa's best and brightest to become world-class software engineers and technologists. We are a company. For profit. Our developers are full-time employees. They are folks with high levels of persistence, grit, desire to learn, and ability to take feedback"- Seni Sulyman, vice president, global operations at Andela.

Andela's Strategy and business model

According to Christina Sass, co-founder of Andela on growing tech talent in Africa at the Disrupt San Francisco, 2016.

"Andela's business model is that growing tech teams who need extra-ordinary talent hire Andela and they hire us for a full time integrated team member.
They come to us because we can onboard people very rapidly and because of the selection process. We are also consistently listening to Clients' feedbacks and there is a clear feedback loop within the first 6 months of

the fellowship. It is very intensive; it is like masters' level training.….."

In essence, Andela fellows are trained in business soft skills, attention to details, managing complex stakeholders, etc. These are the things companies need to build great products. Andela provides it for them. Andela also focuses on cutting-edge technical skills which makes companies rush to them because they need talents and they need them now. Andela secures contracts from companies like IBM, Microsoft, Facebook and Plural Sight. The Company outsources her talents to these companies who pay Andela; outsourced talents are paid while Andela keeps their commissions. The companies that hire Andela have re-iterated that they do so because of speed, onboarding, ramping up and the quality of talents both in soft skills and technical abilities.

The significance of Andela; why Andela is an Otherish giver.

Andela is an Otherish giver. Not the conventional kind of Otherish giver. Andela is an Otherish giver in 2 stages. Andela services her talents and also companies that recruit them on short or long term basis.

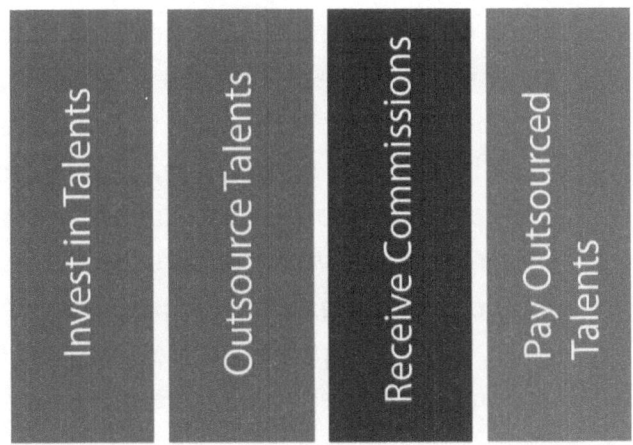

(a) Invest in talents (b) Outsource talents (c) Receive commissions from contract payments (d) Pay outsourced talents.

Andela seeks tech talents (especially Software Engineers), trains and equips them, outsources them, pays them and get her own commissions. The cycle continues.

According to Martin Konicek in his article, *"why demand for software is going to stay high"* posted on the Medium platform on the 11th Oct, 2018.

"The Whole world runs on software: This is probably obvious because it's a transition that's been ongoing for a few generations. However, it cannot be understated. Every single business and organization in the world needs an app or a website plus lots of software, often custom if the company is large. Every person with internet access (which eventually will be the whole world) uses lots of apps and websites every day". This point is to help you understand the scale of Andela's operations.

Furthermore,

"Most things get built many times: Why is there Bing or Mozilla Firefox when there is Google? Why are there a thousand competing e-commerce platforms? Why are there a million messaging apps, each built from scratch by a different team? This seems like the duplicated effort but it's normal. It's just how competition works and it's not unique to software. For example, there are many car companies, each with tens of thousands of employees designing and building very similar cars. Part of the reason is software is still local...."

This is just the beginning of software development. Everybody is directly or indirectly involved in this 'movement'. As long as software development continues to be the future, Andela would keep on rising and expanding. Much more human capacities would be built and as always, there will be ready customers (Companies) to patronize them. I foresee a business to consumer (B2C) approach to be implemented by Andela in no distant time in order to consolidate their standing as market leaders. Growing customers are constant, the growing population is served technology-wise, Andela stays winning. The Company deserves some accolades.

2. **Odunayo Eweniyi**: She is the co-founder and Chief Operations Officer at Piggybank now renamed Piggyvest. This is one non-conventional Nigerian lady I have heard about from friends and the social media.
"......on the last day of 2015, someone shared pictures of her *kolo,* in which she had saved N1000 every day in the calendar year, on Twitter. Immediately, one of Odunayo's co-founders, Josh Chibueze started to look for a way to digitize this concept....
By mid-January 2016, version one of the Piggybank product was ready.
Being the unofficial devil's advocate in the group, Odunayo kept the team honest as they fleshed out their ideas for Piggybank. In no

time, the team had beta-tested version 1 of Piggybank, shut it down, then Paystack launched and by April 2016, a fully launched Piggybank was available to the public". Culled from Akindare Okunola's article for tech cabal titled, Brains, Focus and Grit.

As a self-professed pessimist, she is usually the one questioning everything.

The piggyvest company is on a mission to tackle the almost non-existent savings culture amongst Nigerians. Who would blame Nigerians when 60% of incomes are spent on food. There's hardly anything left to save after deducting transport, shelter and health budgets. In most cases, individuals are already on the negative waiting for the next pay day.

A sustainable business that aims to help people save, invest and grow their incomes have been formed. Piggyvest has an emotional connection to its customers because it is solving a very personal problem. Features such as group savings towards a goal have been introduced. The souls of customers are being motivated when Piggyvest celebrate best savers on the platform and social media on a monthly basis.

Unlike conventional bank savings accounts, the piggyvest restricts withdrawals until an agreed date or users can withdraw their savings on a quarterly basis, whereby savings drawn outside of the agreed day attract a 5% early withdrawal fee. So while the platform is extremely simple and flexible to use, customers are also incentivized financially to keep their money in place, until the agreed date.

User Base Growth

Piggyvest's growth can be attributed almost entirely through peer-to-peer recommendations; verbal endorsement from trusted people within your wider network is a super-powerful mode of marketing. Piggyvest's users are their influencers, their advocates. Africans are storytellers, so piggyvest has applied this tradition, this genetic structure that sits in all of Africans, to build their user base, which has seen a 3000% savings growth between 2016-2017 and 20-35% month on month growth in user traction over the past years. By the end of 2017, Piggyvest had saved 1 billion Naira.

Piggyvest's Revenue Generation

Piggyvest generates its revenues through asset management, and revenue margins currently stand at 4 - 7%. So, every month, users save, and piggyvest invest a portion of that float, and plough back most of the interest they get back to their users. Users earn an average of 6% per annum on automated savings or 10.95% per annum on the fixed deposit product, Safelock, which is higher than the average interests around. Users have since exceeded 100,000 people.

By creating a value system aimed at attacking an endemic problem; the lack of savings culture, the piggyvest company is seeing massive growths in users' retention, peer to peer product recommendation and users' trusts.

Piggyvest is an Otherish giver. The company has given the population a product to help them save and invest their incomes. I will also like to let you know that Piggyvest has acquired a significant stake in a Microfinance bank. Money will be made more aggressively now.

If you would make money from population numbers, give the population what it desires because population is always hungry.

3. **Onyeka Akumah**: He is the co-founder and Chief Executive Officer of Farmcrowdy; a digitized agriculture platform. If you are fascinated by the business of Agriculture but do not possess the grit, luxury of time or know-how to get the 'dirty work' done on the farm? FarmCrowdy is the platform that allows you to engage in the process of Agriculture business right from the comfort of your phones or computers and from anywhere in the world without owning a farmland or being visibly present.

Source: *Twitter*

According to Onyeka's tweet on June, 2019, he said "When we designed Farmcrowdy, we created a model that was never used before in Nigeria for the Agriculture space to fund farm projects. From day one, we started with 1 farmer and today, we have worked with over 11,000 farmers in 14 states across Nigeria and..."

According to FarmCrowdy's blog, FarmCrowdy business model is in two parts.

(a) They identify crops for the farming season, have a farmers' integration process where they work with committed farmers in farming clusters in different communities, provide them with improved seed varieties, training on modern farming techniques and source for off-takers.

(b) They provide a secure platform where individuals sign up for a free account, and select farm units that they want to sponsor. They then use the sponsors' funds to engage the farmer and at the end of the farming cycle, sponsors get their initial sponsorship and returns on their investments.

Problems FarmCrowdy is solving; the creation of value.

Daniel Anuoluwapelumi Moses, a writer and blogger had this to say about FarmCrowdy in 2017.

".....In a study undertaken at the faculty of Agriculture, Ahmadu Bello University in 2013, certain factors were identified that deter youths from participating in Agriculture. You know what excites me the most? Farmcrowdy addresses a number of these factors to a large extent. Stay with me.
According to the study, 39.7% of youths are constrained as a result of inadequate incentives. It points out an obvious fact that Agriculture is not

featured prominently in the media and is rarely glamorous when it is. Lack of incentives could also include inadequate fund available for youths interested in agriculture. This is as reported by Umeh and Odom (2011).

But since the emergence of Farmcrowdy one year ago, I can say that it has become a bit more popular amongst youths. People have decided to turn to the once dreaded agriculture as it can now be done easily, with lesser capital, while making profits too. Farmcrowdy is really making sure.

The research pointed out that almost 30% of youths avoid agriculture because they do not have the adequate training and extension services. The point here now is, Farmcrowdy does not require you to be trained before you can participate in agriculture. All you need is a smartphone, and some funds in your bank account of course and you're good to go...."

Business Structure and Management

They have an experienced management team, technical field specialists and a host of other experienced individuals to ensure the successful operation of the business.

At this point, I presume you must have grasped the Otherish giver's mentality in the FarmCrowdy's business model.

They recognized the need for food sustainability. They move out to source farmers that are interested in food cultivation. They partner them, train and equip them, leverage on the population, and get investments from them to sponsor farmers during farming cycles. The whole procedure ends in food availability, farmers' increased incomes, more dividends for investors on the platform, FarmCrowdy's commissions from the whole process and a win-win situation.

From the Otherish Giver's perspective, Farmcrowdy partners with the population; the investment conduit to solve the problems in the Agriculture sector of the economy. This is made possible using secured technology platform as the distribution channel.

Solve a problem by creating value, have a very low barrier to entry (this still bothers on affordability) for the population; it is not so costly to be an investor on the platform, distribute the value, and make money.

5

Digitalpreneurs' Model

Digitalpreneur is anybody who earns a living by way of their computer or mobile phone. If you scam people by way of your mobile phone or computer, you are a thief that should be prosecuted.

'Digitalpreneurship' is the new trend of entrepreneurship. Online Freelancers, Social media influencers, digital marketers, digital media consultants, digital book publishers etc. all fall under the Digitalpreneur's canopy. The list is endless.

The internet as we know today has broken every barrier to earning good income. I have seen people make money via freelance platforms like fiverr.com doing what they love. I have seen people set up online stores to sell their products without any physical store. I have seen books published and distributed without the obsolete bureaucratic ways via the internet, we all experience people seriously cashing out from making engaging contents on Instagram, Facebook, Twitter etc.

Some popular folks in the Nigerian media scene especially Instagram are Lasisi Elenu, Maraji, Tunde Ednut, Joro etc. These guys are either developing contents or offering services that the population (massive followers) are always ready to pay for.

If you are saddled with an internet enabled phone or a PC, you can make money in today's World. Start freelancing today. Join popular platforms like fiverr and upwork to sell your services and be sure to do so professionally. Start a blog; write on anything you are passionate about, there are tons of the population waiting to read your contents, that is how you would grow your income. Build contents on your social media platforms; Instagram is the best platform right now because it has the right tools to help you make a fortune. Do not waste your time on social media doing bants. If you need more help doing this, you can contact me at dominiquearc007@gmail.com

Digitalpreneurship follows the Otherish Givers' principle of giving and receiving. "...Give, it shall be given unto you, good measures pressed down, shaken together shall men give unto your bosom"..... This is a Bible verse.

When you give value, you will receive money. Digitalpreneurs exchange their values (video contents, writing skills, freelance services etc.) for money. They make more money when they begin to service a significant chunk of the population. Population is hungry. Population is your conduit to experience untold wealth. Give them your service and values. You will make money legally. Welcome to the digital economy!

Source: *www.demandsphere.com*

According to an article on Pixlee.com titled, *what is an Instagram Influencer?* it states that, "an Instagram Influencer is an Instagram user who have an established credibility and audience; who can persuade others by virtue of their trustworthiness and authenticity......."

The above image is that of an Instagram influencer. He loves body building. He does that and uploads the pictures on his handle. He begins to amass followers who can relate to his passion one way or the other. Within 3 to 6 months, he has amassed enough followers to make money from.

How does he make money?

He can be approached by companies who want their products to reach a large audience by leveraging on his handle. OR

He can approach companies he knows might be willing to advertise on his platform. Looking at the picture, he could readily approach fez cap, the wristwatch or the sleeveless hood company to market their brands. He can also choose to market body building related products.

Population is your conduit.

6

Conclusion

The most certain way to make money in any economy by leveraging on the population (numbers) is by being a GIVER. Stop being at the receiving end of values. You are only worth your value at the end of the day.

Find more sustainable ways to scale your giving to a greater chunk of people especially when you must have discovered their pain points.

If you practice the Otherish giver's principle, you will make exceeding cash in any economy.

Now, I guess you know that givers never lack.

It has been my pleasure making an impact. Thanks.

You can reach out to me through dominiquearc007@gmail.com

Call or text me on +2348162002742.

7

Bibliography

https://medium.com/@ameet/be-a-giver-think-of-others-and-get-ahead-9e39010d0284

https://www.lemonade.com/blog/psychology-givers-takers-matchers-2/

https://sheleadsafrica.org/how-one-company-defied-the-odds/

https://www.ntusbfcas.com/african-business-insights/content/consumer/168-tolaram-evolution-in-africa

https://www.conversationagent.com/2017/09/successful-givers.html

https://markets.ft.com/data/equities/tearsheet/summary?s=DANGCEM:LAG

https://www.youtube.com/watch?v=x8OuwUoO-Co

https://www.investopedia.com/articles/investing/100615/how-aliko-dangote-became-richest-african.asp

https://www.voanews.com/africa/nigerias-population-projected-double-2050

https://www.legit.ng/426890-wealth-secrets-of-aliko-dangote.html

https://www.dangote.com/about-us/

https://www.legit.ng/1138476-top-10-fast-moving-consumer-goods-nigeria.html

https://goodkeywords.com/kb/products.php

https://en.wikipedia.org/wiki/Mo_Ibrahim

https://www.youtube.com/watch?v=OBnQ21NSpMw&t=1853

https://www.forbes.com/sites/jordandaykin/2018/12/06/the-millennial-entrepreneur/#50f0a3df7c40

https://smallbiztrends.com/2013/05/millennials-work-and-entrepreneurship.html

https://medium.com/@senisulyman/tia-this-is-andela-33203d10975b

https://www.financialtechnologyafrica.com/2017/07/25/africa-is-where-you-build-businesses-to-maximize-the-next-billion-users-flutterwave-co-founder/

https://techpoint.africa/2019/07/29/how-i-work-odunayo-eweniyi-piggyvest-co-founder-and-chief-operations-officer/

https://www.youtube.com/watch?v=LGbYlfSOozI

https://medium.com/swlh/why-demand-for-software-engineers-is-going-to-stay-high-5acb789c5015

https://techcabal.com/2018/06/08/brains-laser-focus-and-grit-a-profile-of-odunayo-eweniyi-co-founder-piggybank-ng/

https://www.forbes.com/sites/mfonobongnsehe/2018/05/31/meet-piggybank-ng-the-nigerian-fintech-startup-that-just-raised-1-1million/#dec3c4210ca2

https://guardian.ng/news/nigeria/piggybank-asserts-expansion-plans-becomes-piggyvest/

https://blog.farmcrowdy.com/farmcrowdy-twitter-threads-truth/

https://techmoran.com/2017/11/15/farmcrowdy-one-defined-future-agriculture-tech-nigeria/

https://digital-preneurs.com/what-is-a-digital-preneur/

https://www.slideshare.net/garudapreneur/digitalpreneur-76466085

https://www.pixlee.com/definitions/definition-instagram-influencer

https://www.demandsphere.com/blog/instagram-influencers-for-marketing/